Original title:
Spaced Out Sonnets

Copyright © 2025 Creative Arts Management OÜ
All rights reserved.

Author: Elias Marchant
ISBN HARDBACK: 978-1-80567-804-5
ISBN PAPERBACK: 978-1-80567-925-7

The Poetry of Astral Wanderings

In a rocket built from tinfoil bright,
I zoom past planets in the starry night.
The aliens wave, with green thumbs up,
As I sip cosmic juice from a shiny cup.

My cat floats freely in zero-G,
With a look that says, "You should've stayed free!"
She chases asteroids like they're big mice,
While I wonder if space fish might taste nice.

I land on Mars, but what do I see?
A picnic of Martians, all laughing at me!
They serve me moon pies on a platter of rings,
I eat and I munch, my space suit just sings.

Back in my ship, I start to doze off,
Dreaming of moons, where the aliens scoff.
They shout, "Earthling, come join our dance!
But bring your own snacks, we'll give you a chance!"

Soaring on Solar Wings

Flapping through the galaxy bright,
I met a star that thought it could write.
It scribbled across the Milky Way,
But it only drew a coffee stain, I say.

Jupiter's storms, a wild dance,
I tripped on a cloud, thought I'd prance.
But gravity laughed, pulled me down,
I landed quite softly in a space clown.

Celestial Odyssey

Riding a comet, what a thrill,
Dodging asteroids gives me a chill.
I waved to Mars, it winked back slow,
"Watch out for Pluto, it's feeling low!"

Galactic mischief on a donut ring,
I danced with aliens, they could not sing.
Their voices were chirps, a funny sight,
In zero G, we laughed with delight.

Chords of the Cosmos

Strumming stars, I found a tune,
Pluto hummed along, as late as noon.
The Milky Way joined in with a spark,
Even black holes twirled, oh what a lark!

With space kazoos, and moons that clap,
We rocked out loud, in a cosmic rap.
Each planet cheered, "Encore, encore!"
Astronomers puzzled, wanting more.

Reflections in a Celestial Pool

Diving in stardust, what a splash,
Reflections of Venus made quite the hash.
I saw my face in Saturn's rings,
And giggled at all the silly things.

Under the surface where comets drift,
The laughter burst forth, a galactic gift.
"Splash zone ahead!" a sign did say,
Cosmic water fights are the best kind of play.

Whispers of the Milky Way

Stars giggle in bright hues,
Comets dance like they've got shoes.
Aliens with parties held,
Popcorn meteors, all repelled.

Jupiter wears a funny hat,
Saturn spins, just look at that!
Galaxies in merry flights,
Space-time jokes on moonlit nights.

Nebulous Wishes and Dreamscapes

Clouds of stardust float away,
Wishing wells where comets play.
Dreams like astronauts in space,
Faceplanting with style and grace.

Cosmic giggles tickle spheres,
Planets whisper through their cheers.
Echoes of a cosmic tune,
Earthlings yawn and gaze at the moon.

Eclipse of the Heart

When the moon gives a cheeky peek,
Sun's bright light begins to leak.
Hearts collide in a cosmic laugh,
When gravity's math goes daft.

Love notes in the starlit skies,
Asteroids with loving sighs.
A slip of space, they trip and fall,
Meteors share a giggly brawl.

Celestial Cadence

Rhythm of stars in playful spins,
Dancing planets, where fun begins.
Shooting stars play hide and seek,
Lighting the cosmos, oh so chic!

Uranus twirls with a jester's flair,
Venus snickers, light as air.
Wobbly orbits make hearts soar,
In this vastness, we want more.

Celestial Whispers

In a galaxy where cats can float,
Asteroids chase a disco goat.
Stars giggle as they twirl in space,
Moonbeams chuckle, a wobbly race.

Planets wear their silly hats,
While comets dance with silly cats.
Gravity's off in this cosmic play,
As laughter echoes through the Milky Way.

Stardust Serenades

Shooting stars with twinkling eyes,
Sing of space pies and strange fried fries.
Galactic birds wear polka-dot ties,
While giant bugs play the harmonize.

Bouncing moons on pogo sticks,
Spinning around with cosmic tricks.
The universe grooves, a comical vibe,
In this funny dance, we all subscribe.

Galaxies in Bloom

Nebulas bloom like flowers bright,
While space squirrels plot the next kite flight.
Planets giggle under the sun,
As black holes play hide and seek for fun.

Asteroids wear tutus, twirl and sway,
In this goofy cosmic ballet.
Starry friends burst into glee,
In a universe wild, as funny as can be.

Cosmic Echoes of Love

Aliens send hearts from afar,
On rocket ships shaped like candy bars.
Black holes whisper sweet nothings near,
While asteroids toast with cosmic beer.

Between comets, love messily flies,
With glittering dreams that light up the skies.
In this zany realm of joy and charm,
The universe chuckles, holding us warm.

Lullabies from the Nebulae

In the stars, where dreams take flight,
Fluffy comets zoom through the night.
Cosmic giggles fill the air,
As space cows float without a care.

Galaxies wave as they spin around,
Singing tunes without a sound.
Planets bounce on clouds of fluff,
Silly aliens can't get enough.

Moonlit Musings on Mars

A Martian sipped his berry tea,
Wearing socks, oh what a spree!
Dancing rovers, what a sight,
Wobbling left, then leaping right.

Red dust swirls in joyful cheer,
As moonbeams tickle, far and near.
Space potatoes take their stand,
Loudly giggling 'til they're tanned!

The Dance of Distant Stars

Twinkling lights in a waltz so grand,
Stars prance about, hand in hand.
They twirl and spin in baffling delight,
As gravity's rules take the night flight.

Distant suns wear hats to express,
Cosmic fashion that's quite the mess!
Jupiter's juggling, Saturn's in tune,
What a party beneath the moon!

Wandering Through the Milky Way

In the Milky Way I stroll so free,
Dodging meteors just to see.
Chocolate stars drop from above,
As aliens shout, "We want some love!"

Black holes whirl, with a playful grin,
Sucking up socks—they're quite the win!
Nebulae burst in bursts of cheer,
Through the cosmos, laughter's near!

Galactic Flourishes

In a galaxy where socks do roam,
Stars align to find a home.
Planets dance in dapper ties,
While martians wear ridiculous flies.

The sun wears shades, it thinks it's cool,
While moons play hopscotch at space school.
Asteroids crack jokes, oh what a sight,
As comets zoom by laughing in flight.

Reveries of the Universe

Nebulas swirl like cotton candy,
While aliens munch on spaghetti handy.
Galactic fairs with rides astray,
And black holes that open for a sway.

Aliens juggle with stars ablaze,
Laughing together in cosmic play.
With quasars beaming like disco lights,
They dance through the voids, oh what delights!

The Skies Hold Our Secrets

In the night, the stars giggle bright,
Whispering tales of the silly flight.
Mars painted red, wearing a hat,
And Venus just dodging a big flying cat.

Uranus sings bass in cosmic bands,
While Mercury boasts with flashy hands.
The cosmos bounces with laughter galore,
As the Milky Way spins to the floor!

Afloat on Cosmic Currents

Floating on rays of sunshine beams,
Space travel feels like a series of dreams.
Rocket ships painted like bright balloons,
Sail the night sky with gigging tunes.

Shooting stars play hide and seek,
While black holes make you lose your cheek.
Cosmic waves that tickle and tease,
In a universe where laughter is the breeze!

Midnight Comets and Heartbeats

In the night, comets zoom,
Chasing dreams, leaving a plume.
My heart races, feeling light,
As stars giggle, oh what a sight!

They whisper secrets, oh so high,
While I ponder if I can fly.
With a wink, the moon creeps near,
And I chuckle, "Is that a deer?"

Echoes of the Infinite

In space, echoes do a jig,
With voices funny, oh so big.
They bounce back, twist and twirl,
Like cosmic dancers in a whirl!

Each giggle ripples through the void,
A stellar tune we can't avoid.
The stars laugh at the things we say,
As if they know we'll miss the play!

Dancing Among the Constellations

With Orion's belt, I tie my shoes,
Ready to waltz with spacey blues.
A pirouette with the Milky Way,
In a dance where comets sway!

The Big Dipper spills its drink,
While I trip and spill my think.
Stars clap hands, what a sight!
Fumbling through the cosmic night!

Stardust and Shadows

In shadows made of stardust wisps,
I try to catch a few sweet sips.
They tickle me, and I erupt,
In laughter, oops! I've overstepped!

With Saturn's rings around my waist,
I spin and twirl with no real haste.
The universe winks, what a tease,
As I beg for more cosmic cheese!

Poetic Sojourns Among Stars

In a rocket made of cheese, they zoom,
With a mouse as their pilot, they'll find the room.
Asteroids dance while comets giggle,
In zero-gravity, they jiggle and wiggle.

Planets wearing hats spin round with glee,
While aliens sip tea on the rings of a spree.
Stars throw confetti, a cosmic parade,
As cosmic balloons in bright colors cascade.

A space cow sings from a galactic hay,
While moonbeams wrap 'round like a soft ballet.
The sun takes selfies, a shining delight,
In this funny realm where all is just right.

So pack your bags, take a trip in the night,
Where laughter and tales are always in sight.
In the depths of the cosmos, humor's the key,
Join this jovial journey, it's fun and carefree!

Ballad of the Cosmic Winds

Through the nebula's dance, a breeze twirls around,
With a hiccup and giggle, strange sounds abound.
Stars wear their glasses, looking quite daft,
While comets crack jokes and moonbeams laugh.

Clouds of cotton candy drift past like dreams,
Galaxies jive in outrageous schemes.
A space dog barks at a comet's long tail,
While Martians make muffins and sing a sweet tale.

Planets spin stories of wild, whirling bliss,
In the theater of void, they share a big kiss.
Black holes play hide and seek with delight,
As they twinkle and wink in the velvety night.

So let the cosmic winds carry you away,
To a land where it's fun and laughter holds sway.
With each swirling trip, discover the whims,
Of the universe's song and its playful whims!

Eclipsing Echoes

When the moon and the sun have a playful stare,
They tiptoe around, a cosmic affair.
Stars whisper secrets of funny goodbyes,
As they blink to each other with mischievous eyes.

A shadow takes shape, making faces of glee,
While aliens gather for giggles and tea.
Solar flares tickle, causing a fit,
As Jupiter jumps, doing a backflip split.

Galactic echoes send laughter on high,
Bouncing off planets as they curtsy and sigh.
Supernovas bloom like flowers of jest,
In this universe, humor is truly the best.

So listen for jokes in the cosmic ballet,
Where joy spins the stars in a whimsical sway.
Join the dance of the echoes, where laughter ignites,
In the sweet symphony of celestial nights!

Twinkling Tales of Time

In the clockwork of stars, odd stories arise,
Where time takes a break to enjoy silly ties.
A wink from a galaxy, a giggle from Mars,
While Saturn spins round in its polka-dot jars.

Time-traveling snails take their sweet, funny stroll,
Joking with comets, making laughter their goal.
Each tick and each tock, a punchline so grand,
As the universe chuckles, oh isn't it planned?

Chronicles swaying with whimsical grace,
In the fabric of time, there's joy to embrace.
Past and future meet in a delightful ballet,
As they tease each other in a celebratory way.

So gather your winks and chuckle with glee,
Join this funny trip through eternity.
With the twinkling tales lighting up the sky,
Embrace humor's magic that never says die!

Of Planets and Poets

On Mercury, poets write with speed,
They rhyme so fast, they plant a seed.
Venus laughs with her clouded grace,
While Mars just wants a little space.

Jupiter sings in a booming tone,
His storms like verses, wildly grown.
Saturn's rings are a poet's dream,
With icy whispers and a gleam.

Uranus rolls with a tilted style,
His sonnets leave us all in a smile.
Neptune dives deep in ocean blue,
Writing lines that feel so true.

All these worlds in cosmic play,
Poets dance on the Milky Way.
With every line, they spin and twirl,
In the great galactic whirl.

Chasing Celestial Fireflies

In the night sky, fireflies dart,
Chasing sparks and a cosmic art.
A comet winks, a starlet giggles,
In this chase, the stardust wiggles.

Galactic fun in the twinkling light,
We catch a wish on this magical night.
With laughter bright, we swirl around,
As every bounce brings a silly sound.

Planets peek from behind the haze,
In this lively, starry maze.
Each little flicker brings a cheer,
As the universe lends us its ear.

So catch a firefly, but don't be shy,
Let the galaxy be your merry sky.
For in this dance of light and bliss,
Even the cosmos can't resist.

Luminous Parables of the Night

Under moonbeams, stories unfold,
With tales of planets brave and bold.
A shooting star trips on a rhyme,
As night giggles, passing the time.

In the quiet, comets share,
Whispers of love in the chilly air.
Asteroids chuckle as they collide,
Bringing laughter on this cosmic ride.

The Milky Way spins in delight,
Its glittering dance, a joyful sight.
Every star a character, bright and sly,
In this whimsical tale written high.

Join the fun in this celestial game,
Where every world's a bit insane.
For in the sky's embrace and light,
We find parables in the night.

Interstellar Rhapsody

Echoes of laughter roam the void,
In the cosmos, silliness enjoyed.
Nebulas swirl in a colorful haze,
Giving rise to laughter's praise.

On asteroids, we bounce and play,
With space dust tickling all the way.
Blasting tunes from suns so bright,
Creating joy in the flight of night.

Galaxies hum a silly song,
While laughter echoes all night long.
In this rhapsody, we're all a part,
Celestial harmony warms the heart.

So raise a toast to the stellar crew,
In this dance of cosmos, just me and you.
For every twinkle is a wink from fate,
In the universe, let's celebrate!

Annuals of the Astral

In a galaxy filled with sparkly trash,
Asteroids dance in a cosmic bash.
Planets wobble, they giggle and sway,
While comets throw parties, hip-hip-hooray!

A space whale swims in a milky expanse,
Singing to stardust, the universe's dance.
With alien jokes that make moons revolve,
Who knew the cosmos had such a solve?

Black holes munch on galaxies with glee,
Devouring starlight like it's candy.
Martians throw pies, aiming for fun,
In a tangle of laughter, they lose track of the sun.

So here we orbit, in joyful delight,
Making wishes on stars that twinkle at night.
For in the vastness, we're never alone,
With humor and joy, we've happily flown.

Shadows of Distant Worlds

Beyond the stars, with laughter anew,
Planets giggle as they spin and skew.
Saturn's rings jingle like a wild parade,
While moons throw confetti that never will fade.

On Jupiter's storms, a playful tornado,
With lightning strikes putting on quite the show.
Neptune wears shades, looking oh-so-cool,
While Pluto insists it's still part of the school.

Distant galaxies share the cheekiest memes,
A cosmos where humor intertwines with dreams.
Eclipses have punchlines that always surprise,
And comets delight with their glittery ties.

So raise a toast to the mirth up high,
In the celestial realm where laughter won't die.
With shadows that dance in the light of the night,
The universe chuckles, expanding our sight.

A Voyage Through Solar Winds

In a rocket shaped like a giant cheese,
We soar through the cosmos, a cosmic breeze.
Solar winds tickle as they sweep us away,
With laughter igniting the light of the day.

Aliens sipping juice in their strange spaceships,
Swapping wild tales, and exchanging cool quips.
They teach us to dance with stars by our sides,
As we glide through the galaxy on joy-filled rides.

Meteor showers burst into fits of cheer,
As we dodge silly asteroids flying near.
Our mission? To make the universe smile,
While spinning in circles, laughing all the while.

So let's journey onward, with whimsy as our guide,
Navigating the cosmos, with laughter as our tide.
In this voyage of fun, adventure so grand,
We find joy in the vastness, hand in hand.

Harmonizing with the Stars

Under a moon that sings, our tunes collide,
Stars offer rhythm, dancing in pride.
With instruments crafted from cosmic debris,
We jam with the planets, it's wild and free.

Galaxies swirl, conducting the fun,
As supernovas burst, their fireworks spun.
The Milky Way hosts a jazz-loving crowd,
Where every black hole plays loud and proud.

On Venus, they hula, in gravity's sway,
While Martians play charades in a cosmic ballet.
The cosmos is swelling with harmony bright,
A symphony echoing through the starry night.

So let's strum the strings of the heavens above,
In a playful duet, with laughter and love.
For in this grand concert that sparks the divine,
We're all just stardust, and it's truly fine!

Reflections from a Distant Sun

A glow from afar, quite bizarre,
It tickles my senses, a cosmic guitar.
The stars chuckle low, like they know '
Why the moon sometimes wears, an old disco flow.

My thoughts drift along, a comet's bright tail,
Spilling laughter like stardust, on a grand scale.
Planets play tag, in a celestial race,
While aliens sip tea, with a cheeky face.

The sun winks and beams, a radiant prank,
Making shadows that dance, like ships in a tank.
In this universe mad, full of glitter and fun,
Who knew that light years could make us all run?

So here's to the giggles, from stars far and wide,
To the quirks and the laughs that the cosmos provide.
Reflections of joy, light-years away,
In this grand galactic cabaret we sway.

Chronicles of Interstellar Muses

In a dance with a quasar, I twist and shout,
Each twinkling star, a muse to flout.
Galactic silliness, in the midnight air,
Where black holes burp, without a care.

Who knew asteroids could juggle so well?
With laughter that echoes, a spacey hotel.
Nebulas swirl, like cotton candy fluff,
In this playful realm, things aren't too tough.

Comets come crashing, with glittery glee,
They high-five the planets, as they fly free.
With cosmic crayons, we paint the dark sky,
Each stroke a giggle, as we zoom on by.

So pen down your tales, of the madness we find,
Among celestial jesters, beautifully intertwined.
The universe laughs, with a twinkle and tease,
In the chronicles penned, where whimsy's the sweet breeze.

Echoes Through the Cosmic Canopy

Whispers of laughter float on space winds,
Echoing loudly where the star dust begins.
Mars pulls a prank, with a wink of its eye,
As Saturn spins tales through its rings that fly.

Galaxies giggle, in outlandish delight,
While meteors glide, painting paths in the night.
Moonbeams wear hats, and the stars wear masks,
In this absurdity, who needs questions or tasks?

The comets and planets, they dance like a band,
And Pluto plays spoons, with a trembling hand.
Nebulae sing out, a hilarious tune,
Making jokes with the sun, while plotting to swoon.

So let's frolic through wonders, both silly and grand,
In the cosmic canopy, where humor is planned.
For echoes of laughter, across the great blue,
Are the finest of treasures in this vast view.

Celestial Ballads in the Infinite

In the realm of the stars, a ballad begins,
Led by giggling planets, as each one spins.
Jupiter croons under its stormy old shrouds,
While Venus spins tales that draw giggling crowds.

Cosmic cats prance, with tails curled just right,
As rockets do cartwheels in the soft starlight.
Time bends like ribbons in this endless dance,
Where the laughter of quasars offers a chance.

Galactic sultans in robes made of space,
Joke about light-speed with a quizzical grace.
Comets slip by, chuckling sweet nonsense,
A symphony of silliness in cosmic expanse.

So raise up a toast, with juice from the sun,
To those splendid ballads, where all's just for fun.
In the tapestry woven through laughter and light,
Forever we twirl, in the dance of the night.

Harmonic Celestial Journeys

In my rocket, I took flight,
Until I hit a star too bright.
Thought I'd land on Jupiter's moat,
But I splashed down in a giant boat.

Pluto waved, said, 'Take a seat!',
His icy snacks were quite the treat.
We danced through rings of Saturn's gold,
While telling tales of days of old.

Uranus rolled with laughter loud,
As Mercury chimed, proud in the crowd.
They all agreed, I had great style,
But tripping over space dust? Just my trial!

In the end, we formed a band,
Playing tunes of stars so grand.
With cosmic rhythms, we'll not tire,
Galactic grooves, we'll never retire!

Constellation of Dreams

A shooting star fell from above,
Said 'Hey there!', like a cheeky dove.
I caught it in a coffee cup,
Now it bounces, won't shut up!

We sketched a map of zigzag lines,
Connecting all the best designs.
Orion danced a silly jig,
Fell right over, oh so big!

The Milky Way spilled cosmic wine,
Hosting parties, oh so fine.
I wore a costume made of space,
And twirled like I was in a race!

Each dream a spark, each laugh a tune,
We partied hard beneath the moon.
In this funny realm of stars,
We'll paint the night, just me and Mars!

A Symphony of Space

The trumpet of a comet blew,
A cacophony that felt brand new.
I grabbed a seat on Saturn's ring,
To jam with stars, such a wild fling!

Neptune sang with a fishy voice,
While Venus clapped, oh what a choice!
We harmonized through asteroids,
Avoiding space rocks—what a void!

A black hole spun a funky beat,
We boogied hard on our little feet.
With every note, the cosmos swayed,
Creating vibes that never frayed.

When the encore came, what a sight!
Galaxies danced in sheer delight.
Each funny sound and silly cheer,
Made space a stage, oh so dear!

Rhythm of the Stars

Underneath the twinkling lights,
Planets gathered, ready for fights.
Mercury, fast, took the lead,
While Mars joked about planting seed.

Asteroids clashed, creating sounds,
Rhythms echoed all around.
Even the sun joined the crew,
Flapping its rays, as if it knew!

The moon played hide and seek with night,
While stars twinkled, oh what a sight!
Cosmic dancers spun and twirled,
In this funny, wacky world.

As the song faded, we shared a smile,
In this universe, let's stay awhile.
With laughter echoing, we declare,
The rhythm of space, beyond compare!

The Starlit Path of Memory

Once I lost my keys in space,
They floated off without a trace.
A cosmic search amid the stars,
To find them near the moons of Mars.

Asteroids laughed and danced around,
As I twirled, a space-bound clown.
Each comet winked, a playful jest,
While aliens cheered for the quest.

I tripped on Saturn's rings one night,
Fell headfirst, oh what a sight!
But then I laughed, all pain forgot,
In the vast and silly cosmic plot.

So now I roam the stellar scene,
A memory lost, yet so serene.
With cosmic giggles, I invite,
Join me on this starlit flight!

A Tapestry of Celestial Sighs

In a galaxy filled with cheese,
I found a mouse, oh what a tease!
He built a rocket from a slice,
Said, 'I'm off! The stars are nice!'

With every bite, the planets spun,
Making space travel so much fun.
In the Milky Way, we danced,
With every crumb, our fate enhanced.

The sun hummed songs, oh so sweet,
While asteroids brought us tasty treats.
We hosted a feast on Mars' red dust,
For cosmic pals, it was a must.

So here's to laughter up above,
Crafting dreams we so dearly love.
In this tapestry, let's unwind,
For every giggle, peace we find!

Whispers Across the Universe

The stars were gossiping one night,
About a cat that took flight.
He soared past Jupiter's great storm,
In a space suit, decidedly warm.

He landed on a comet's tail,
With tales of fish that never fail.
Those space-bound whispers danced away,
As Earth sat quietly in dismay.

Aliens cracked up, what a view!
A cat in space, who would've knew?
They cheered and laughed, creating cheer,
Echoing giggles from ear to ear.

So when you feel a cosmic breeze,
Know it comes with laughs and ease.
For whispers through the void embrace,
The funny antics we can trace!

Thank You for the Stars

Thank you stars, you shine so bright,
Guiding me through this silly night.
With every twinkle, you remind,
To laugh and dance, not just unwind.

I caught a shooting star on a dare,
But it turned out to be my hair!
Space jokes like these, they bring such glee,
Reminding us of lightness, you see?

With rockets made from paper planes,
We zoomed through nebulae like trains.
A cosmic ride, far from the cars,
With laughter echoing through the bars.

So here's a toast—to fun and cheer,
To memories made across the sphere.
Thank you, stars, for every laugh,
In this vast and wacky cosmic path!

Horizons of Hopes and Stars

On a rocket made of cheese,
We zoom past Jupiter with ease.
Wormholes twisting in a dance,
Aliens laughing at our chance.

Floating cats in spacesuits grin,
While astronauts just sip their gin.
A comet's tail brings cotton candy,
Each bite's a taste that's truly dandy.

From Mars, we send friendly tweets,
To Earthlings with their tiny feats.
In zero-G, we do a flip,
Our laughter makes the starships tip.

Galaxies giggle, cosmos cheer,
As we munch on snacks without a fear.
Exploration's quite the jest,
In the universe, we're truly blessed.

Luminescence Among Dark Matter

In the void, we play with rays,
Dancing shadows, silly ways.
Neon stars, they wink and shine,
Making our goofy selves divine.

Black holes giggle, spinning fast,
As we trip on stardust cast.
Quasars flash in cosmic lights,
While we wear our space pajamas tight.

Meteor showers, whirling fun,
We play tag with the blazing sun.
Dark matter hides but loves our games,
As we blast-off with silly names.

Supernovae pop with cheer,
As we toast with space-made beer.
In laughter lies the universe,
With every joke, the stars immerse.

Dreamscapes on Cosmic Waves

We surf the waves of milky foam,
Riding comets far from home.
Galactic tides that ebb and flow,
Bring surfboards made of moonlit glow.

Asteroids become our stage,
As we perform with cosmic rage.
Shooting stars take double takes,
Applauding all our wild mistakes.

Nebulae swirl in cotton hues,
While we sip on starlight brews.
Gravity's punches make us laugh,
We float around like silly gaffs.

In this dreamy astral space,
We skip and jump with boundless grace.
Our laughter tickles planets near,
In this vast void, we persevere.

Rhythms of the Celestial Sea

Beneath the suns of sapphire blue,
Mermaids play with aliens too.
Galactic waves roll with a splash,
As we surf through the cosmic thrash.

Neptune's whales sing silly songs,
As planets hum along all day long.
With a bounce, we join the tune,
In this ocean, we're all immune.

Shooting stars, like fish, we catch,
In nets of laughter, quite a match.
Gravity's tickle makes us swirl,
As starfish wink and woodwinds twirl.

Dancing on the waves of night,
We twirl with meteors in delight.
In this celestial sea, so vast,
The joy we share is meant to last.

Celestial Reveries

In the sky where comets glide,
A cow jumped over, took a ride.
Stars winking like they know a joke,
While moons giggle, giving hope.

Planets dance in silly pairs,
Jupiter wears mismatched flares.
Asteroids sing with rhyming schemes,
As Saturn dreams of ice cream beams.

Neptune's bubble bath is grand,
Mars juggles rocks with careful hands.
Galactic pranks, they laugh and spin,
While space whales dive, they twirl and grin.

Look up high, let worries flee,
The cosmos holds their glee for free.
In this realm of laughter vast,
The funny stars are unsurpassed.

Galaxies of Whimsy

A snail in space, oh what a sight,
Racing stars in the dead of night.
With rocket shells that shine so bright,
He wins the race—what a delight!

Floating fish in zero-g,
Singing songs of galactic glee.
They tickle orbits, splashing fun,
As Saturn spins—oh, what a run!

Zany aliens toss green pies,
While lasers shoot from their bright eyes.
They dance on rings, a wild parade,
In bizarre dreams, the fun is made.

Asteroids roll with silly grins,
While Martians make their goofy spins.
In galaxies where whimsy reigns,
The universe laughs with no refrains.

Stardust Dreams Unfurled

Upon a comet, fairies play,
With twinkling lights in disarray.
They toss stardust on the moon,
And hum a cosmic, silly tune.

A giant cat floats by and sighs,
Beneath the veil of twinkling skies.
He chases tails of meteor trails,
While cosmic mailmen ride on whales.

Planets giggle, spin and sway,
As rubber ducks come out to play.
In fluffy clouds of cotton candy,
They surf the stars, oh isn't that dandy?

In this dream where laughter swells,
Each stardust tale delights and tells.
Unfurled above, the merry scene,
Of funny dreams where space is keen.

Cosmic Whispers and Echoes

Echoes of laughter trail the light,
A cosmic party dances bright.
Whispers from space, a silly sound,
Where joy and jokes can be found.

Dancing moons in polka dots,
Jovian vibes and tie-dye spots.
Singing spaceships with their crew,
Paint the night with colors bright and new.

Black holes giggle, pulling pranks,
While starlings line up in great ranks.
Foggy nebulae laugh and swirl,
As the universe gives a playful twirl.

In this theater of the bold,
Funny tales of space unfold.
With cosmic whispers, laughter glows,
In a galaxy where joy just flows.

Moonscapes of Solitude

In craters deep, I bake a pie,
With starry friends who laugh and sigh.
The moonbeams dance, they twist and twirl,
While aliens join in a cosmic whirl.

A comet's tail is now a mop,
Cleaning up each lunar plop.
We throw moon rocks like they're confetti,
As space cats play, all light and petty.

Space snacks float in zero G,
Tacos drift by, just like a spree.
With giggles loud, we share a bite,
In our own world, all day and night.

Galactic tunes we strum and sing,
On asteroid drums, each note will swing.
In silent space, our laughter rings,
With moonscapes bright, oh what joy brings!

Light Years to Your Heart

A spaceship built from cardboard dreams,
Zooms past the stars with silly beams.
Through galaxies of giggles loud,
I chase your smile, of that I'm proud.

With space maps drawn in crayon bright,
I'll find your heart, my guiding light.
Navigating through the cosmic jest,
In this wild ride, I am the best.

Asteroids dodge like pesky flies,
As I shoot for you, no need for ties.
In rocket shoes, I leap and bound,
To find your love in this vast surround.

Each light year brings a chuckle bold,
With tales of warmth on nights so cold.
In all this space, my heart does chart,
A funny quest to win your heart.

Cosmic Lullabies

Singing stars in twilight's glow,
Whisper tales of joy and woe.
A nebula spins like a curly fry,
As I hum soft, oh my, oh my!

Space kittens frolic in sunbeam threads,
As I tuck in my dreams in cozy beds.
The Milky Way's a bedtime tale,
Where cosmic jokes are never stale.

Floating through a dreamy track,
With comets racing in my pack.
In the stillness, giggles rise,
As the moon winks with sleepy eyes.

Each twinkling star, a lullaby soft,
In this galactic world, we drift aloft.
With smiles stitched in the cosmic skies,
We find our peace, alongside these ties.

The Universe in Verses

In every rhyme, a planet spins,
With quirky facts and silly wins.
A playful sun with a cheeky grin,
In this vast verse, we laugh and spin.

The stars are bright, but wait a second,
Did Pluto leave? Oh, time to reckon.
Each line we write is light as air,
With puns that float, we have to share.

Galaxies bloom like flowers rare,
In the cosmos, joy is everywhere.
We scribble words in cosmic jars,
And even dance with twinkling stars.

In this universe, our antics play,
With every verse, we've found our way.
So let the worlds collide in fun,
With silly thoughts for everyone!

Enchanted by the Cosmos

Stars waltz in the night sky,
Twirling like dancers with grace.
I thought I saw a comet,
But it was just my neighbor's vase.

Galaxies giggle, they spin,
Jokes hidden in their vast light.
I aimed my telescope high,
Found a cat chasing the night.

Planets are playing hide and seek,
Oh, what a cosmic game!
I cheered for my favorite moon,
But it just looked back with shame.

In this quirky universe,
Laughter floats on solar breeze.
If you trip on a black hole,
At least you'll land on your knees!

Love Letters Written in Light

In the glow of the moonlight,
I scribble sweet cosmic notes.
The stars are my paper,
And the comets, my floating boats.

Your smile is a shooting star,
Dashing across my heart's sky.
I sent you a love letter,
But it got stuck in Mars' flyby.

I penned a lullaby for you,
While winking at a bright quasar.
But it sang back a silly tune,
About finding my lost car.

Cosmic love feels so surreal,
Like gravity's tugging at my toes.
Every wink from Venus is sweet,
Except when she steps on my nose!

Mosaics of the Universe

Crafting mosaics of starlight,
With colors that make me grin.
A nebula's rainbow in sight,
Oh look! A splatter of gin!

Each piece tells a story untold,
Of quirks in a cosmic parade.
Like aliens trading their gold,
For a good cup of lemonade.

Saturn wears stunning new rings,
While Jupiter shows off his flair.
I bet they have grand parties,
With asteroids dancing in the air.

In this odd celestial craft,
I find humor woven tight.
For even the black holes chuckle,
When they swallow a delightsome bite!

Beyond the Event Horizon

I peered past the event horizon,
Into a realm of silly fate.
Where time takes a coffee break,
And space-time laughs till late.

Space monsters play hide and seek,
Hiding in the shadows of stars.
They tickle the backs of comets,
While stealing their candy bars.

Black holes become cosmic clowns,
Juggling planets like they're gum.
But when they trip, oh my dear friend,
It's a planetary ransom!

I float in this absurd ballet,
Where laughter echoes through the void.
Out there in the cosmic sea,
Even the aliens seem overjoyed!

Through the Galaxy of Dreams

In a ship made of marshmallows, we fly,
Past planets that giggle and starry pie.
A comet sneezes, what a sight to see,
As aliens play twister, oh what glee!

We skip on the rings of Saturn with flair,
And dance on the moons like we haven't a care.
With jellybean stars and a chocolate sun,
We laugh as we race, oh this is such fun!

A black hole opens, but we're not concerned,
For cosmic ice cream is what we discerned.
We'll take a scoop, then zoom right along,
Through the vastness where laughter is strong!

With each little wobble of our silly ship,
We jostle and juggle, taking a trip.
To visit the worlds where giggles abound,
In a galaxy of dreams, joy can be found!

Navigating the Ether of Existence

With a map drawn in crayons, we sail through the void,
Dodging space squirrels who seem rather annoyed.
Their acorn torpedoes, oh what a plight,
Yet their tiny shouts echo in pure delight!

Our captain, a cat in a cosmic space hat,
Holds the wheel steady while playing with that.
A dashboard of buttons plays polka and funk,
While asteroids dance like they're part of the junk.

Through stardust and giggles, our journey is long,
We stop for a treat; it's a hot dog song!
With ketchup stars and mustard that shines,
We munch and we laugh, oh, life is benign!

As satellites twirl like marionettes,
We paint the whole sky with our funny pets.
In the ether of existence, we find our way,
With laughter and joy, we'll always stay!

A Symphony of Celestial Bodies

In the orbits of rhythm, we groove and we sway,
With planets that jive, they lead us astray.
A moon with a trumpet sends out a sound,
While comets on saxes are flying around!

Jupiter's drumming, it's quite offbeat,
But Saturn's hey-ho makes it all neat.
Each note from the cosmos is oddly sublime,
Like a dance party held at the edge of time!

Stars with their shimmer are part of the band,
They twinkle in sync, isn't it grand?
We clap with delight at this cosmic charade,
In a symphony where no one's dismayed!

From a sunbeam solo to a black hole's bass,
This quirky ensemble gives joy to the space.
And while planets may wobble and space may astound,
We laugh through the music, in laughter, we're found!

Twilight in the Asteroid Belt

At twilight, we wander this quirky old belt,
Where asteroids chat and strange feelings are felt.
One rock wears a top hat, how dapper he seems,
While others play marbles and share funny dreams!

A meteor shower is reading the news,
And planets gossip with playful witticues.
With laughs and jests, the twilight plays on,
Underneath a pizza-shaped moon, we have fun!

We dance with the dust and waltz with the light,
Collecting the giggles that twinkle at night.
Every bump of a boulder brings chuckles galore,
In this twilight realm, who could ask for more?

So let whispers of starlight wrap us in cheer,
As we journey in laughter, let joy steer!
Through the asteroid belt where time takes a rest,
In twilight's embrace, we are truly blessed!

Astral Dreams and Distant Stars

Atop a comet, they sip their tea,
With biscuits made of stardust, oh so free.
They giggle at the planets spinning round,
In this absurdity, joy is found.

Whispers from the asteroids, quite loud,
Congratulating Earth for making a crowd.
Jupiter's storms dance a silly jig,
While Saturn's rings fit a disco wig.

Cosmic critters in the Milky Way,
Form a conga line, come what may.
Galactic roller coasters twist and twirl,
In laughter, and fun, they all unfurl.

The Moon plays hide and seek with sun,
While comets race just for the fun.
Astral architecture, a madman's dream,
Wonders of the universe, it does seem.

Voyagers in the Void

Light years from home, with snacks galore,
They dance on meteors and glide on floor.
Spaceships honk and bump in style,
Joyful noise rings across each mile.

Aliens in tutus hop and twirl,
While planets do their cosmic whirl.
With each strange noise, a giggle escapes,
Even black holes make funny shapes.

On Jupiter's moon, they play dodgeball,
With gas giants watching, laughing for all.
Stardust sprinkle gives off a glow,
As they take turns, watched by a crow.

In the void where echoes chase their tail,
They find the humor in the pale.
Each adventure a funny tale told,
In a universe vast and bold.

Nebulae of Nostalgia

Twinkling memories float through the haze,
Icons of laughter from younger days.
Floating like cotton candy dreams,
In cosmic corners where nothing teems.

Faded photos from a time long past,
Chase shooting stars and dance fast.
Backyard rockets made from old cans,
Countdown to fun with our own silly plans.

Bubblegum nostalgia, sweet as can be,
With planets bouncing like a trampoline.
Silly faces made from starry dust,
In the universe's playground, we trust.

Time machines made of cardboard and tape,
Crafted by kids with a simple shape.
Traveling through a nebula so bright,
We laugh at the cosmos; it's pure delight.

Celestial Ballads

Singing songs to the rhythm of space,
With notes that shimmer and embrace.
The stars join in with a twinkling hum,
As planets bounce and tap their drum.

Melodies of mischief, a joyful sound,
Floating through the cosmos, spinning around.
A chorus of laughter rings through the night,
While aliens stomp their feet in delight.

In the starlit glow, a party unfolds,
With snacks from quasars and tales retold.
Each verse a step, each note a dance,
In our cosmic cabaret, we prance.

Comets flicker like vibrant lights,
As we sing with joy through endless nights.
In this universe of absurd and fun,
Celestial ballads shimmer and run.

Time Travelers in Tattered Pages

In dusty books, the whispers fade,
Where clumsy time machines have strayed.
A knight in shorts, a ghost in a hat,
They journey back with a squeaky brat.

With every flip, a coffee stain,
A wizard laughs, then trips on chain.
The clock ticks back, but pants won't fit,
They giggle loud, as pants all split.

They raced through time in crazy shoes,
A dodo bird gave them the blues.
The past is funny, though quite a mess,
When history wears a fruitcake dress.

So when you read, just look and see,
The notion of what could never be.
A unicorn with a lizard's grin,
We'll laugh at time as it wears thin.

Fragments of a Distant Galaxy

From galaxies bright, they send a text,
A selfie with aliens, oh what's next?
They wear silly hats and dance around,
In every pic, pure chaos found.

A comet zips by with a silly face,
While space cows mooo in zero grace.
Juggling stars like balls of light,
They tumble down in a galactic fight.

With supernova fries and moon pies,
They laugh out loud as the rocket flies.
For cosmic jokes are best in space,
Where time is wobbly, at a fast pace.

And if you see a twinkling star,
Just know it's laughing, from afar.
Fragments of joy in a cosmic spree,
Come join the fun, it's meant to be!

Pathways of the Soul

Through silly paths, the souls do dance,
Wearing mismatched socks at every chance.
A wobbly waltz on the edge of fate,
Their giggles echo, so don't be late.

With heart-shaped donuts and jellybeans,
They skip along with uproarious scenes.
Every step, a chuckle, quite profound,
In realms where laughter knows no bounds.

With colorful wings, the spirits fly,
In zany hats, they wave goodbye.
A tickle of joy in every twist,
In pathways of the soul, you can't resist.

So dance with glee when the spirits meet,
In every laugh, feel the joy repeat.
For a journey of fun, we'll elegantly stroll,
In whimsical pathways to uplift the soul.

Secrets in the Starlight

Under starlit skies, the secrets flow,
With whispers soft, in a twinkly show.
A raccoon sings with a voice so sweet,
While owls dance to a funky beat.

The moon, a jester, playing tricks,
With shadows that do somersault flips.
A marshmallow comet zooms on by,
With giggles hidden in the night sky.

In every glimmer, a wink and sigh,
The galaxy holds mysteries high.
Like socks that vanish in the wash,
Starlight chuckles, hey, who's the posh?

So gaze above and let out a laugh,
At secrets shared in starlit craft.
For under the cosmos, dreams take flight,
With giggles wrapped in the soft, warm night.

Eclipsed by the Silence of Space

In cosmic halls where echoes fade,
My thoughts get lost, like socks in a raid.
Stars giggle softly, twinkling bright,
While I ponder why cats can't get flight.

Floating thoughts drift, oh what a mess!
Are aliens just shy, or playing chess?
I ask the moon why it shines so wide,
It whispers back, 'Just enjoy the ride!'

Do black holes swallow pizza too?
Perhaps they crave a pepperoni view!
Galaxies dance, their rhythm's a tease,
While I trip on stardust, oh, if you please!

The sun's a giant lamp, burning bright,
Yet I still wear shades, just to be polite.
In spaceships, we'd laugh with glee,
While dodging meteors, sipping free tea!

The Heartbeat of Comets

Comets zoom by with tails of ice,
Whispering secrets, oh so nice.
They bounce on waves of solar wind,
While I juggle planets without a spin.

I shared a sandwich with a star,
It said, 'Next time, please bring a car!'
Galactic picnics, such a delight,
But ants in space just don't seem right.

My friends are meteors, quick on the go,
They blaze through skies, putting on a show.
I chase them round like a puppy's thrill,
Oh, to catch a comet, what a skill!

In this wild space, laughter's our tune,
We dance with planets, beneath a full moon.
With giggles that echo through the night,
The universe shimmies, oh what a sight!

Celestial Journeys Beyond the Sky

A rocket powered by jellybeans,
Zooms past all the earthly scenes.
With a crew of squirrels, sharp and spry,
They plot their voyage to the big, blue sky.

They count the stars like chocolate chips,
Inventing games on cosmic trips.
'Watch your head, there goes a star!'
'Told you to dodge, we're flying far!'

Planets wave as we pass them by,
One winked at me, oh my, oh my!
The galaxy giggles, a grand parade,
With meteors dancing, unafraid.

Floating through space, a true delight,
Squirrels with helmets, oh, what a sight!
Every journey sparks a new laughing spree,
On our silly quest, just you and me!

Fragments of Light in Infinity

Shattered starlight scattered wide,
Each twinkle a wink, a cosmic guide.
I caught a beam, thought it was cheese,
But it rolled away like a dandelion breeze.

Riding rays of laughter through the haze,
Infinity's jokes can leave me amazed.
With each cosmic giggle, I feel so light,
Even aliens can't dim this delight!

Pieces of light, a puzzle so bright,
They scatter like confetti in the night.
I reach for a star, it giggles, then flies,
'You can't catch me, silly, I'm wise!'

So here in the cosmos, we play and we sway,
With joy in abundance, come what may.
From the tiniest spark to galaxies wide,
In this funny universe, we take a ride!

Soliloquy of a Shooting Star

In the sky, I zipped and zoomed,
A wish got lost, now I'm marooned.
Chasing dreams like they were kites,
But now I'm just a streak of lights.

I tripped on clouds, oh what a mess,
Thought I'd land in fame, I guess!
But here I am, a cosmic joke,
Winking at Earth, a shining bloke.

With giggles echoing through the night,
I flicker, sparkle, a silly sight.
Do they know I'm passing by?
Just a star who forgot to fly!

So make a wish, toss it high,
But don't expect me to comply.
I'm just a wanderer, full of cheer,
A cosmic clown, swinging near!

Harmonics of the Universe

In the cosmos, I strum a tune,
With planets dancing, oh what a boon!
Satellites waltz in a celestial jig,
While comets twirl, looking quite big.

Neptunes play trumpet, Mars hums bass,
Galaxies swirl in a cosmic race.
I burst out laughing with each note,
As stars burst forth from twilight's coat.

Asteroids drop, a rhythm so wild,
While black holes giggle, like a playful child.
The universe cheers in perfect pitch,
We're all just notes, in this cosmic glitch.

So turn up the volume, let laughter reign,
In the harmonics of space, you'll never complain.
Join the dance, let spirits rise,
In this silly symphony, under bright skies!

Serenades from the Silent Cosmos

In silence, the stars hum a tune,
Their melodies drift like balloons.
Singing softly, they play their parts,
Whispering secrets from distant hearts.

The moon joins in with a cheeky grin,
While meteors race, hoping to win.
Cosmic jokes in the vacuum's play,
"Did you hear what the sun did today?"

With twinkling eyes, they share their mirth,
Laughing together, for all they're worth.
A serenade that's oddly sweet,
As starlight dances, I tap my feet.

So tune in to this galactic show,
Where silence speaks, and giggles grow.
In the vast expanse, take a seat,
Join the choir, life's truly neat!

The Language of Starlit Nights

Under the stars, I speak in jest,
With moonbeams lighting my weird quest.
"Hey there, Venus, how's the glow?"
"Not too bright, just putting on a show!"

The cosmos giggles, so vast and wide,
With Saturn's rings, like a roller coaster ride.
I slip and slide on Jupiter's cheer,
The laughter cascades, oh, so dear!

Pluto shouts, "I'm still a player!"
While asteroids shout, "See ya later!"
The language of night is a jokester's dream,
With laughter echoing in the cosmic stream.

So if you glance up, don't be shy,
Wave to the stars, give a little sigh.
They might just wink back, in the dance of light,
In this funny tale of a starlit night!

Orbital Love Songs

In orbits wide we twirl and spin,
With love notes sung like rocket engines.
You stole my heart with cosmic flair,
Now starlit giggles fill the air.

Your eyes, two moons that softly glow,
They light the way when tempests blow.
We dance on rings of Saturn bright,
In space, my dear, we're quite the sight.

Our kisses launch like shooting stars,
Creating smiles on distant Mars.
With laughter echoing through the void,
In this vast realm, we're overjoyed.

So take my hand on this wild ride,
Let's spin around the universe wide.
In every laugh, a galaxy shines,
In orbited love, our hearts entwine.

Legends of the Luminous Night

The moon whispers tales of winks and cheers,
As we float through space, defying fears.
Meteors trail our giggly flight,
In legends sung beneath the night.

You're my comet, sleek and bright,
Dashing by with pure delight.
Our laughter fills the endless dark,
In shooting stars, we find our spark.

Cosmic jesters with hearts on fire,
Create a symphony of desire.
In nebulas of joy, we dive,
Together here, we come alive.

With each new supernova's bloom,
We dance through space, dispelling gloom.
In this vast realm of endless flight,
We craft our legends of the night.

Playgrounds of Planets

On Jupiter's swings, we giggle and play,
With Saturn's rings, we float away.
In cosmic parks, we chase the stars,
Building sandcastles on fiery Mars.

Venus has slides that spiral high,
Where laughter echoes in the sky.
Pluto's corners hold secret charms,
Just wait till you see those cosmic farms!

We race through asteroids, dodging debris,
Crafting a ruckus, just you and me.
In the playgrounds of space, we are free,
With starlight tickles and glee aplenty.

So grab my hand, let's spin around,
In our universe, pure joy is found.
With every laugh, we spin anew,
In this cosmic playground, it's me and you.

Tides of Cosmic Passion

In moonlit waves, our hearts collide,
With cosmic tides, we take a ride.
Under nebulae, we spark and twine,
In this universe, you are divine.

The stars align, creating waves,
Pulling us closer, like ocean graves.
We surf on beams of vibrant light,
With every laugh, we soar to new heights.

Through cosmic tides, we freely flow,
With each embrace, the galaxies glow.
In this vast sea of stardust dreams,
Our passion blooms in radiant beams.

So let's dive deep where comets roam,
In this universe, we find our home.
With every tide that pulls us near,
Our cosmic love sings loud and clear.

Songs from Beyond the Horizon

In the sky, a cow did fly,
With a moonlit laugh and a wink of an eye.
Stars misplaced in a game of chess,
Who knew they'd cause such a cosmic mess?

Jupiter sings with a lopsided grin,
While Saturn shakes hands with a mischievous pin.
A comet slipped on a banana peel,
Leaving a trail that looked quite surreal.

Aliens dance with their legs in the air,
Chasing the notes of a cosmic fair.
With every twirl, they startled the sun,
Whose rays turned to giggles – oh, what fun!

So raise a glass to the stars above,
And toast to the strange things we dearly love.
For in this vast and silly expanse,
Every planet's a stage for the galaxy's dance.

Stellar Stories Untold

A Martian told a tale so grand,
Of a rubber chicken in a distant land.
It bounced through time like a wayward kite,
Landing on Pluto, late one night.

Venus flipped pancakes in zero-G,
While Mercury played the trombone with glee.
The asteroids joined in a wild dance,
Spinning and swirling in a cosmic prance.

Neptune wore socks that did not match,
Swapping with Uranus, what a catch!
Their style was noted across the Milky Way,
A fashion faux pas that still holds sway.

So gather 'round for tales from the skies,
Of quirky galaxies and starry pies.
With laughter ricocheting through the void,
These stellar stories can't be destroyed.

Harmonies of the Heavens

In a land where the stars hum a tune,
Earth's cats debate the merits of the moon.
A supernova cracks jokes with a grin,
While black holes are busy, swallowing in.

Twirling comets are on a swing,
As meteors join in, ready to sing.
Pluto's off-key but dances with pride,
While Mercury wins every cosmic ride.

From Venus, the flowers throw confetti in air,
As Andromeda giggles, without a care.
Galaxies whirl in a joyful embrace,
Learning to laugh in the vast, open space.

So tune in, dear friends, to the celestial beat,
For the universe's chorus is simply a treat.
With harmonies bright, and humor so bold,
These tales of the heavens are treasures untold.

Orbits of Longing

A spaceship lost its way to the mall,
Forgetting the planets had fun after all.
With asteroids playing hide-and-seek,
They found a comet who couldn't speak.

Saturn's rings were a hula-hoop dare,
While Mars flipped burgers, showing great flair.
The sun joined in with a solar flare,
Sizzling up burgers for everyone there.

Black holes laughed at their gobbling fun,
Suggesting desserts from the great big sun.
As Venus served ice cream, a delightful scoop,
They danced in orbits, a merry troop.

So mark the stars on your cosmic map,
For laughter and snacks can bridge every gap.
In the grand dance of the universe wide,
It's the joy in the journey, not just the ride.

Cosmic Connections in the Void

In a galaxy not quite so far,
Aliens chat with cheese from a jar.
They play cards with stars in hand,
And laugh at their own cosmic band.

Black holes joke, 'Let's take a trip!'
While comets glide on a quirky slip.
Mars wears shades, looks rather cool,
While Pluto says, 'It's always a duel!'

Neptune's mood swings, quite a drama,
Uranus chuckles, 'What's your karma?'
Together they mingle, a cosmic spree,
In the universe, how silly they can be!

Echoes of laughter through infinite space,
Galactic goofballs, a comical race.
Dancing with meteors, stars twinkle bright,
In the void they find their own light.

A Tapestry of Cosmic Thoughts

Saturn's rings sing a playful tune,
While Jupiter grins, 'I'm the biggest balloon!'
Stars gather round for their cosmic feast,
Where black holes serve spaghetti at least.

Shooting stars wish for quiet nights,
But they trip on space dust, oh what sights!
Cosmic crayons color the sky so wide,
While stardust giggles in playful pride.

Milky Way wraps all in a hug,
While meteoroids seek a cozy rug.
Galaxies swirl in a merry waltz,
Sharing secrets with no cosmic faults.

Laughter echoes in ethereal chambers,
Creating moments the mind remembers.
In this tapestry where dreams collide,
The universe laughs with joy and pride.

Orbiting Melodies of Time

Planets with rhythm, they start to sway,
Dancing to a beat that's far, far away.
Asteroids rock to a cosmic jam,
While Saturn's rings are like a shiny glam.

Time ticks in sync with comet delight,
As they pirouette through a waltzing night.
Lightyears bound, but jokes move fast,
Mirthful moments in a cosmic blast.

Venus hums a sassy pop tune,
While Mars plays peek-a-boo with the moon.
Time zones collide with a giggling twist,
In the orbit of laughter, none can resist.

Through the vastness, melodies cheer,
Every twirl brings the universe near.
For in this dance of celestial rhyme,
Time spins hilariously, oh so sublime!

When Planets Kiss the Horizon

When planets meet, it's quite the sight,
They blow kisses in the fading light.
Stars gossip about who wore what,
While the comets sport a dazzling dot.

Mercury whispers sweet nothings fast,
While Venus beams, keeping secrets amassed.
Uranus grins as it rolls on by,
Saying, 'Watch me spin, oh my, oh my!'

Jokes are exchanged around the sun,
As Earth chuckles, 'We're all just one.'
Astrological quirks and cosmic pranks,
Fuel the friendship in their celestial banks.

The horizon blushes with colors unbound,
As laughter and joy swirl round and round.
In this grand gala, the cosmos conspires,
To paint the sky with infinite wires.

www.ingramcontent.com/pod-product-compliance
Lightning Source LLC
Chambersburg PA
CBHW051651160426
43209CB00004B/872